Rediscovering Caesarea Philippi:

THE ANCIENT CITY OF PAN

Rediscovering Caesarea Philippi:
THE ANCIENT CITY OF PAN

Edited by John F. Wilson

Pepperdine University Press
Malibu, California

Published on the occasion of the exhibition "Rediscovering Caesarea Philippi: The Ancient City of Pan,"
at the Frederick R. Weisman Museum of Art, Pepperdine University, Malibu, California. The exhibition
was jointly sponsored by the Pepperdine University Institute for the Study of Archaeology and Religion
and the Israel Antiquities Authority.

Printed and bound in the United States of America

ISBN 0-932612-26-1

Front cover: Coin of Marcus Aurelius (No. 129)
Inside front cover: Artist's rendering of Banias Basilica

Design of catalogue: Heidi Lundgren and Pepperdine University Publications office
Photography: Tsila Sagiv (courtesy of the Israel Antiquities Authority)
Illustration: Shalom Kweller
Design of exhibition: Dorit Harel
Plans courtesy of the Israel Antiquities Authority
Printed by Haagen Printing

TABLE OF CONTENTS

The nineteenth-century village of Banias

FOREWORD

In 1988, when the site of Caesarea Philippi/Paneas was officially designated as a nature reserve, the Israel Department of Antiquities (now the Israel Antiquities Authority), with the cooperation of the Nature Reserves Authority, decided to begin methodical excavations to rediscover the ancient city.

Later, the Government Office for Tourism also joined the project. Two large-scale excavations were organized. The first, designed to excavate the cave of Pan and the temples surrounding it, was placed under the direction of Dr. Zvi Maoz. The second, designed to explore the central area of the site, was assigned to Dr. Vassilios Tzaferis. This second project, which became known as the "Joint Expedition," involved a consortium of universities that provided professors and student volunteers. Dr. John F. Wilson, representing Pepperdine University, served as director of this consortium. Other participating institutions included Averett College (Danville, Virginia), led by Dr. John Laughlin; Southwest Missouri State University (Springfield, Missouri), led during various seasons by Dr. Victor Matthews, Dr. Charles Hedrick, and Dr. LaMoine DeVries; Hardin-Simmons University (Abilene, Texas), led first by Dr. George Knight and later by Dr. Don Auvenshine and Dr. Don Williford; Abilene Christian University (Abilene, Texas), led by Dr. John Willis; Kapodistrian University (Athens, Greece), led by Dr. Nicholas Olympiou; Concordia Seminary of Indiana, led by Dr. Charles Gieschen and Dr. Arthur Just; and Howard Payne University (Brownsville, Texas), led by Dr. Don Auvenshine.

The current exhibition, "Rediscovering Caesarea Philippi: The Ancient City of Pan," provides the first opportunity for the public to see the results of twelve years of work at the site. The exhibition is sponsored by Pepperdine University,

FOREWORD

with the help of a number of generous donors and the active cooperation of the Israel Antiquities Authority. We particularly wish to thank Amir Drori, former director of the IAA, for his support and encouragement. The overall design is the work of Harel Designers of Jerusalem (Dorit Harel, Director). Special thanks goes to Shoshana Israeli, deputy director of the Joint Expedition, for her crucial assistance, and to Ruta Peled of the IAA. A representative selection of artifacts has been chosen from the thousands that have come to light during the excavations in order to give some idea of the long history of the city, encompassing two millennia and several major cultural transitions. The history of Banias (the modern name for the site) is deeply rooted in the histories of all three of the great religions of the region: Judaism, Christianity, and Islam. It is thus fitting that the staff and the workers involved in this project represent an impressive multicultural array: Americans, Greeks, Israelis, Arabs, and even the Druze villagers from nearby.

Special thanks are also due to Marne Mitze, director of Pepperdine's Center for the Arts; Dr. Michael Zakian, director of the Frederick R. Weisman Museum of Art; Claudia Arnold, assistant vice chancellor, and her staff and colleagues at Pepperdine University; and all those individuals and organizations who have encouraged this project with their support. We also think with affection of the thousands of citizens of Banias, who for two thousand years lived their lives, dreamed their dreams, and occasionally lost or left something behind, thus enabling us to share their world. Imagine their surprise if they knew that, through these humble artifacts, they have become a part of the history of the new world as well!

THE HISTORY
by John F. Wilson

THE HISTORY

ROMAN CAESAREA PHILIPPI

The cave, red-rock cliff, and springs at Banias first appear in history as the "Panion" in the writings of Polybius around 200 B.C.E. The name indicates that the place was already identified with the Arcadian god Pan, who was worshiped at caves in various places throughout the Hellenistic world. With the coming of Rome, Augustus Caesar gave the territory, including Banias, to Herod I (in 23 B.C.E.), instructing him to bring it under Roman law and order. The region was to remain more or less under the control of Herod's family for more than a century.

Herod, according to Josephus, "erected to him [Augustus] a very beautiful temple of white stone . . . near the place called Panion."[1] Josephus describes the cave, the springs below it, and a deep pool within it, calling the site a "most celebrated place." The coins of Herod's son, Philip, minted at Banias, provide some idea of the appearance of this temple. Philip inherited his father's northeastern territories and ruled over them for several decades (to 33 C.E.), establishing his capitol, called "Caesarea Philippi" at the Panion.

Numismatic evidence proves that the era of Banias begins in 3 B.C.E. There is no archaeological evidence of residential areas existing during Philip's reign. It is likely that Banias served as an administrative center for a large number of villages surrounding it.[2] It was during this time that Jesus and his disciples visited the area, as recounted in the famous passage in the Gospels.[3]

Philip died in 33 C.E., leaving no direct heirs. In 37 C.E., Caligula granted Philip's nephew, Agrippa I, his uncle's territories, including Banias. Claudius named Agrippa I's son, Agrippa II, king of the principality of Banias in 53–54 C.E.[4] It was Agrippa II who transformed Banias from a relatively simple administrative town into an impressive Greco-Roman city. "The natural beauties of Panion have been enhanced by royal munificence," says Josephus, "the place having been embellished by Agrippa at great expense."[5] Among the embellishments were probably improvements to the Cardo and, at a later time, the construction of the palace. During the Jewish War (66–70 C.E.), Agrippa and the Jewish population of Banias remained loyal to the Romans. The Jewish community was thus saved

[1] Josephus, *Antiquities of the Jews*, XV 10,3 (363).

[2] Cf. the wording of Mark 8:27, "the villages of Caesarea Philippi."

[3] Mark 8:27–30; Matthew 16:13–20.

[4] Josephus, *Antiquities of the Jews*, XX 7,1 (138).

[5] Josephus, *The Jewish War* III: 514.

THE HISTORY

from annihilation, living in the relative safety of their own quarter in the city. After Nero's death, Agrippa enjoyed a special relationship with the new emperor, Vespasian, whose son, Titus, fell in love with his half-sister, Berenice. After the fall of Jerusalem in 70 C.E., Titus brought the Roman army to Banias, where large numbers of Jewish prisoners perished in games.[6] When Titus succeeded his father as emperor (in 80 C.E.), he tried to make Berenice his empress but found this unacceptable to the Roman establishment. She presumably spent the rest of her life as "Queen of Banias." Agrippa died sometime near the turn of the century, and his little kingdom was absorbed into the Province of Syria.

Though no longer a royal capital, the second and early third centuries were prosperous ones for Banias. The city's name was changed during the

The site of ancient Banias

[6] Josephus, *Antiquities of the Jews*, VII 23–24; VII 37–38.

second century, "Caesarea Philippi" becoming "Caesarea Paneas" or "Caesarea Paniados." The immense royal palace underwent extensive remodeling, which transformed it into a public bathhouse. Under the Antonines the Sanctuary of Pan was enlarged, with the addition of shrines, statues, and inscriptions. The Banias mint produced coins depicting Pan, Zeus, and Tyche. Even more imperial attention was drawn to Banias during the "Syro-Lebanese Dynasty" established by Septimus Severus (193–211 C.E.). Strong trade connections existed between Banias and Tyre, in particular, as well as Damascus and other Hellenistic cities of the area. Coins and inscriptional evidence suggest that the Roman city reached its pinnacle during this dynasty and that the cult of Pan was especially favored during the reign of Elagabalus (218–222 C.E.).

The recent excavations have begun to reveal the town plan of Greco-Roman Banias. The city center was divided into two parts: a "Sacred District" along the base of the cliff, and public buildings such as the bathhouse, a market, and a theater to the south. The *Cardo Maximus*, paved with large basalt stones, ran north-ward on a line that culminated with a view of the Cave of Pan. Under the streets and buildings an elaborate system of tunnels and channels delivered water to the city center, feeding the fountains and pools of the bathhouse and other structures. Some of these still carry water. It is certain that the city had facilities for athletics, and that the "Panion Games" were held there, though as yet these facilities have not been found. Outside the city center the affluent citizens built fine villas among the fields. The middle and lower classes lived mostly in nearby villages.

Despite its essentially pagan nature, a substantial Jewish community existed in Roman Banias, particularly after the Second Revolt, when certain of the rabbis settled there. References to the city in rabbinic literature are rather frequent. It was considered for ritual purposes to be at the northern limit of Eretz Israel and the source of the River Jordan.

BYZANTINE TIMES: THE CHRISTIAN CITY (FOURTH–SIXTH CENTURIES)

Christianity probably arrived in Banias very early, not long after the visit by

THE HISTORY

Jesus himself. The first reference to Christians in the city occurs in the list of participants in the Council of Nicea (325 C.E.), attended by "Philokalos of Paneados." Banias became one of ten bishoprics in the Province of Phoenicia and a fine church was built there. Archaeological evidence suggests that the pagan Sanctuary of Pan only gradually declined, however, rather than coming to a sudden end.

The city became a center of Christian pilgrimage during the Byzantine period thanks to its possession of a famous "Statue of Christ." This statue is first mentioned by an eyewitness, Eusebius of Caesarea.[7] The bronze statue, claimed by the local Christians to have been a votive given to the city by the woman whom Jesus healed of hemorrhage, stood, when Eusebius saw it, "at the gates" of the woman's house. The statue, not mentioned before the fourth century, and in fact not known to the citizens of Banias before that time, was moved for protection into the local church. The church that served as the repository for this statue was undoubtedly the one discovered by the Joint Expedition. It stood in the center of the city, opening onto the *Cardo Maximus* opposite

the remains of the Sanctuary of Pan.

We have little contemporary literary information concerning Banias from the fifth century on. The archaeological record, as discovered by the Joint Expedition and other excavations and surveys, indicates a decline in population and in law and order by the middle of the fifth century. In addition to social and political factors, natural disasters played their part in this decline. Serious earthquakes occurred in the region in 502 C.E. and 551 C.E.

MEDIEVAL BANIAS:
FORTRESS TO ISLAMIC VILLAGE

The "orientalizing" of Syria-Palestine began before the arrival of Islam, initiating the process by which the Greek *polis* was transformed into the Middle Eastern *madina*. Streets became narrower, the large public squares were filled with residences and shops, and the large public buildings were transformed. Eventually these structures became quarries or foundations for structures of very different purpose. Banias did not disappear entirely during this time, but it did enter a period of obscurity that lasted for almost four centuries. Central Palestine came under Arab

---

[7] Eusebius, *History of the Church*, VI 18.

control in 634 C.E., and in the following year Damascus fell. Finally, at the Battle of the Yarmuk in 636 C.E., the Byzantines were driven out of Syria altogether. The significant battles leading to these events occurred quite close to Banias.

During the Abbasid period (750–868 C.E.) the region fell into anarchy and chaos. The eighth and ninth centuries were characterized by revolts and tribal warfare. Christian pilgrimage came to a complete halt. The Moslem writer al-Ya'qubi (891 C.E.) identifies the town as the capital of al-Golan. He calls it *madinat al-askat* ("city of the tribes"), probably indicating that it had become a market town (village?) for a primarily nomadic culture. The monumental buildings were in ruins. The fragments of statues still lying about the Pan sanctuary were gathered up and buried.

The town experienced a rebirth in the second half of the tenth century as Jewish and Moslem refugees from Cilicia filled the town. Among those refugees were many Sufi ascetics, radical Sunnis, who soon made the place a center for resistance against the Shi'ite Fatimids, who now ruled Egypt. This Sufi community at Banias,

said to have miraculous powers, fomented political opposition and theological opposition to the regime in Egypt. Ibn al-Nabulusi, their leader, transformed Banias into an important Sunni educational center. Students gathered from as far away as Iraq to study Hadith under him. His school survived to the beginning of the eleventh century. During this time, Banias' fertile cotton and rice fields caused it to be called the "Granary of Damascus."

The Jewish community in the city called it "Fort Dan," and indeed for the next four hundred years the site functioned primarily as a fort. During the eleventh century, there was a thriving Jewish community in Banias that is frequently mentioned in documents dating from this period in the Cairo Geniza. The small basilica found by the Joint Expedition in the city center may have once served as their synagogue. The Jews seem to have left Banias in the wake of the Crusader successes in the early twelfth century.

THE CRUSADERS: TWELFTH–FOURTEENTH CENTURIES

With the coming of the Crusaders, "Fort Dan" took on new strategic

THE HISTORY

importance. In order to keep Banias in Moslem hands, the ruler of Damascus gave the city to the Ismai'li sect popularly called "the Assassins." Later, fearful for their lives, the Assassins turned the city over to the Crusaders in exchange for safe passage elsewhere. The Crusaders controlled Banias from 1129 through 1132 C.E., when a Moslem army surrounded the city and undermined its walls, causing them to collapse. The defenders fled to the citadel inside the city that had been built directly on top of Agrippa's old palace, but they were finally forced to surrender. Later the Crusaders took the city again and lived on good terms with the Moslems until the "Holy War" of Nur ed-Din (1146–1174 C.E.). The Moslems captured the city in 1164 C.E. Despite several attempts, the Crusaders never held the town again.

Artist's rendering: fountain and pool in the palace of Banias

THE HISTORY

Following the death of the great Moslem leader Saladin (1193), Banias functioned at times as almost an independent state, ruled by his relatives, particularly Al-'Aziz 'Uthman, who became "Lord of Banias." He rejuvenated the city and built a powerful fortress to protect it (now called "Nimrod's Castle"). In 1253, Louis IX sent an army of Crusaders to attempt to take the city. The account of their exploits is preserved in delightful detail in Joinville's "Life of St. Louis."[8]

The disappearance of the threats posed by the Crusaders and the Mongols gradually deprived the town of its military importance, however. With the disappearance of the Crusaders themselves, Western knowledge of the town disappeared as well. Not a single Western traveler left clear evidence of having seen the place until the beginning of the nineteenth century.

MODERN REDISCOVERY

Credit for the site's modern rediscovery is usually given to Ulrich Jasper Seetzen, a German representing the Emperor of Russia, who visited the site on Monday, January 27, 1806. During his visit of three days, he explored the "little hamlet of about twenty miserable huts," the walls of the old fortress, the grotto with its cave and fountain, and the inscriptions along the red rock cliff. He noted the presence of "panthers, bears, a prodigious quantity of wild boars, foxes, jackalls, antelopes, bucks, wolves, hyaenas, hares, etc."[9] Eventually Banias became a staple attraction for western tourists and was visited by everyone from King Edward of Great Britain to Mark Twain. In 1920, following the establishment of the British and French Mandates, the town was placed under French control. Two decades after the collapse of the mandates and the beginning of the modern Syrian and Israeli states, following years of tension and border violence, Banias was occupied by Israeli troops on Friday, June 9, 1967. Soon thereafter, all but its religious buildings were destroyed. In the 1980s the scientific survey and excavation of the ancient city began, resulting in the discovery of the artifacts displayed in this exhibition.

---

[8] Joinville, "The Life of St. Louis," *Joinville & Villehardouin: Chronicles of the Crusades*. Trans. M. R. B. Shaw. New York: 1963.

[9] Seetzen, Jasper Ulrich. *A Brief Account of the Countries Adjoining the Lake of Tiberias, the Jordan, and the Dead Sea*. Bath: 1810, p. 16.

THE SITE
by Vassilios Tzaferis

THE SITE

The excavations at ancient Caesarea Philippi/Paneas (known today by its Arabic variant "Banias") have revealed significant remnants of all the historical periods of the city's long existence—from the second century B.C.E. to 1967 C.E. Zvi Uri Maoz excavated the area of the springs, the cave, and the terrace along the cliffs during the years 1988–1993. There he discovered the Sanctuary of Pan with all its components, such as terraces, temples, prayer courts, and ceremonial spaces. The ceramic, numismatic, and epigraphic finds discovered in this area, as well as the collection of statues, have facilitated the reconstruction of the history of this famous sanctuary from the time of its origin in the late third century B.C.E. until the fourth century C.E., when it was abandoned and destroyed. The surveys and soundings at the site, conducted by Moshe Hartal from 1986 to 1999, identified the residential quarters of the Roman and Byzantine Paneas and mapped the route of the aqueducts that supplied fresh, drinkable water to the northwestern suburbs of the city.

The investigations undertaken from 1988 to the present by the Joint Expedition (see Forward) have con-centrated on the inner organization of the civic and administrative center of ancient Caesarea Philippi and exposed several of its public buildings. The evidence provided by all these archaeological projects, taken together, provides a general understanding of the city plan of Caesarea Philippi, as it existed during the reigns of Philip and Agrippa II. They have also thrown considerable light on what became of the city in Late Roman and Byzantine times, as well as on the nature and function of the town as a fortress during the days of the Crusaders and Ayyubid/Mamluk periods.

We now know that first century C.E. Caesarea Philippi occupied a relatively small space (about 150,000 square meters)—bounded on the north by the springs and the high cliffs standing above them, on the west by Hermon brook, and on the south by the rivulet of the Sa'ar. So far there is no evidence of any significant residential quarter within that area, or even beyond the streams. Thus we conclude that when the Tetrarch Philip founded "Caesarea Philippi" in the year 3 B.C.E., it was not strictly speaking a "city" at all, but rather simply an administrative center where he could carry on the business of his

THE SITE

The Cave of Pan and the source of the Jordan River

THE SITE

kingdom and hold court[1]. This administrative center became a real Greco-Roman city during the second half of the first century C.E., when King Agrippa II, says Josephus Flavius, "embellished the place at great expense,"[2] erecting impressive new public buildings and monuments.

The most impressive structures of the first century C.E. discovered thus far in the excavations include the Colonnaded Street (or *Cardo Maximus*), which bisected the city from south to north, and the remnants of a monumental colonnaded building, located at the northern terminal of the *Cardo* and the royal palace, which dominated the southwest corner of the city.

The palace was undoubtedly the most impressive structure in the city, not only because of its grand dimensions but also because of its sophisticated building style, unique plan, and its creative use of the natural topography. The apsidal halls, the magnificent basilica, vaulted passageways, and impressive interior entrances and exits all suggest consummate architectural and engineering planning and skill, extending to the finest details. After the death of Agrippa II (around the end of the first century C.E.), Caesarea

Philippi was transformed from a royal capital into a provincial town. As such, Paneas retained its status as a *polis*, with all the juridical and social privileges accorded by the Roman regime to Greco-Roman cities. This transition did not result in any major change in the city's outward appearance. It did, however, necessitate modifications in the functions of some of its public buildings. The outward appearance of the palace was preserved, for example, but the inside of the building was converted into a huge public bathhouse. The entire southern wing of the palace seems to have become a series of *caldaria* (heated rooms). Everywhere we excavated we encountered the hypocaust systems that are typical of such installations.

The most significant change that occurred at Paneas during the second and third centuries was the extension of the city limits beyond the streams of Sa'ar and Hermon and the creation of suburbs for private dwellings beyond those boundaries. The new areas stood above the level of the springs; thus, new sources of water were needed. These were found on the western slopes of the Golan Heights. From there an aqueduct

[1] Josephus, *The Jewish War II*, ix, 168

[2] Josephus, *The Jewish War III*, 514

THE SITE

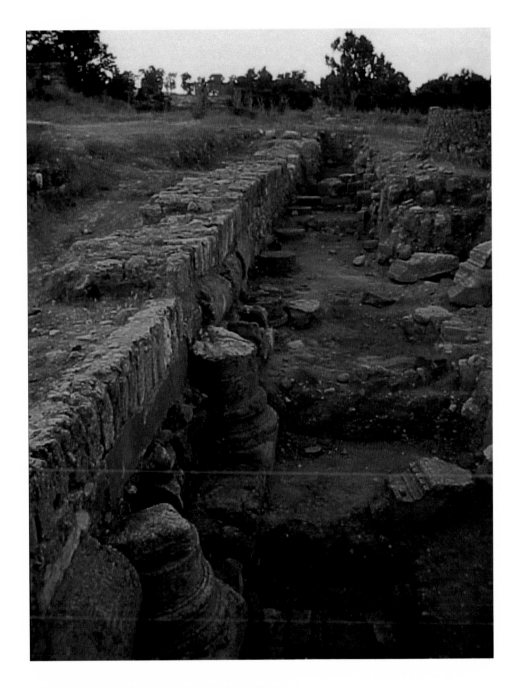

The *Cardo Maximus:* main colonnaded street of the ancient city

THE SITE

more than three kilometers long was constructed to provide a flow of fresh water to the new suburbs.

Caesarea Paneas (as the city was now called) shared in the prosperity that characterized almost all the Greco-Roman cities in the eastern Roman Empire during the second and third centuries C.E. The new aqueduct and the huge bathhouse complex required considerable funds and the presence of skilled personnel. Other signs of affluence appeared. The magnificent palace basilica that in the first century had probably served as a royal audience hall was remodeled, and its interior was covered with beautiful wall mosaics. Fine marble statues representing various deities of the Greco-Roman pantheon were imported in order to enrich and embellish the monuments of the city, particularly the chapels and temples along the base of the cliff. Several new cult spaces and small temples were added to the Sanctuary of Pan, dedicated to deities associated with the god, such as Echo, Hermes, Maia, Nemesis, and others. The coins of the mint at Banias depict some of these

Student volunteers excavating the palace

THE SITE

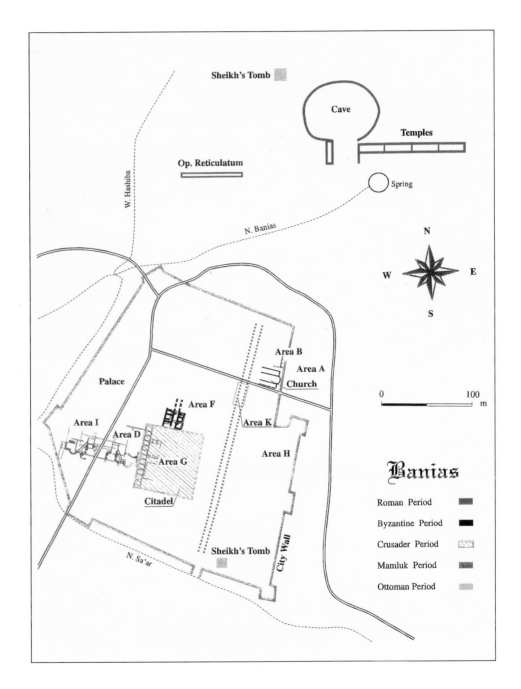

Schematic plan of Roman and Byzantine Banias

deities. The cult of Tyche (the goddess of good fortune) received its first permanent temple. Another temple was erected to Zeus-Jupiter, god and father of both the gods and the human race, probably during the second half of the second century.

These early centuries, from the late first century B.C.E. to the end of the third century C.E., seem to have been the most glorious ones for Banias. The archaeological discoveries from the Byzantine period (fourth to sixth centuries) reveal a city in decay and a society in regression. The great Sanctuary of Pan declined and in the course of the fourth century was abandoned and finally destroyed. Other pagan monuments were either intentionally demolished or transformed to meet the needs of the new Byzantine administration and the new faith, Christianity. The splendid secular basilica in the palace/bathhouse was destroyed, either by some natural disaster or purposely by the Christians of the town. Its architectural elements, pedestals, and columns were then reused in the construction of another basilica erected expressly for Christian worship.

Christian basilica
(See isometric reconstruction on front inside cover.)

THE SITE

The large Christian basilica was constructed on top of a pagan colonnaded building that had previously been completely destroyed. The Byzantine builders of the church reused numerous elements of this earlier structure, such as fragments of columns, decorated architectural elements, and ashlars. The new Christian church was a large and grandiose building, standing close to the springs and just opposite the Sanctuary of Pan. Its location, size, and magnificence symbolized both the decline of the old traditional cult of the city and the triumph of the new faith.

In addition to being a place of worship, the church also became a Christian holy place and a site for pilgrimage. One of its rooms probably housed and exhibited the famous "Statue of Jesus" mentioned by the church fathers.

Soon after the erection of the basilica, however, some calamity seems to have befallen the city. Perhaps this was a matter of social decay, or the aftereffect of a natural disaster such as an earthquake. The discoveries in the so-called "Byzantine Street" in Area F point to the second possibility. The street, flanked on its western side by a

Medieval synagogue/mosque

series of shops and on the east by an elegant public building, was entirely destroyed by conflagration. The latest of the ceramic finds and coins found above the burned floors of the shops are dated to the end of the fourth or the very beginning of the fifth century.

Whatever the reasons, the days of glory for Caesarea Philippi were past. In the ensuing historical periods life continued at Paneas, first as a small town called by the Arabs "Banias," then as a formidable fortress named "Bellinas" by the Crusaders, as an Ayyubid/Mamluk fortified town, and finally as an insignificant Ottoman/ Syrian village.

Among the most interesting archaeological discoveries at Banias from medieval times are the synagogue/mosque found in Area E (dated to the eleventh to twelfth centuries), the Crusader citadel located above the ruins of the palace, and the Ayyubid/ Mamluk fortifications, many of which can be seen above ground to this day. The Ottoman and Syrian village was razed to the ground after the Israeli-Syrian War in 1967.

Objects from the burned Byzantine "Street of Shops" *in situ*

THE ARTIFACTS
by Shoshana Israeli

THE ARTIFACTS

Artifacts discovered during the excavations at Banias include statues; pottery vessels such as lamps, bowls, and jugs; and objects made of metal, glass, bone, etc. Some of these were luxury items and others were simply designed for day-to-day use. They date from the Roman period to modern times (the Syrian village).

These artifacts tell us much about life in the city of Banias during its 2000-year history. They provide evidence of the commercial ties the city enjoyed and something of its economy (the production of ceramic vessels during Roman and Byzantine times, for example, and the manufacture of glass objects during the Middle Ages). They reveal the range of social and economic classes in the city, the various occupations of the inhabitants, and their religious and cultural values. Some remind us of the sometimes violent events that occurred there (the spearheads, for example, and the so-called "pomegranates" or "hand grenades").

FROM DISCOVERY TO EXHIBITION

The artifacts in this exhibition are a small sample of the thousands that have been discovered at Banias. Once these discoveries were removed from the ground, they were subject to a long process of conservation, restoration, and scholarly analysis. First they were cleaned and registered in the field. Then they were sent to various laboratories where technical experts provided further cleaning and restoration. Drawings were made and photographs taken. Only then were the objects ready for display. Thus, the highly skilled staff of the Department of Preservation of the Antiquities Authority partnered in this project.

THE FINDS FROM THE TEMPLES

Working on behalf of the Antiquities Authority, Zvi Maoz excavated the complex of temples and sanctuaries beside the famous Cave of Pan. Many artifacts were recovered from the sacred buildings along the base of the cliff and nearby spring.

Among the most dramatic was a refuse pit where numerous fragments of statues had been thrown. These statues once stood in the sanctuary itself. Five of the better-preserved fragments are displayed. These include life-size heads of Athena wearing a helmet (No. 1), Zeus or Asclepios (No. 2), and body fragments of a statue of Artemis (Diana), whose

THE ARTIFACTS

No. 1

No. 6

No. 2

Marble statues from the excavations

THE ARTIFACTS

head, unfortunately, was not preserved. A miniature head may depict the likeness of an emperor (NO. 4), and a fragment of a hand holding a syrinx or flute may well represent Pan himself (NO. 5). Ancient sources tell the story of how he pursued a forest nymph named Syrinx. She was so frightened by his grotesque appearance that she asked her father to transform her into a reed so that she could hide from the goat god. The disappointed Pan carved a flute for himself from a marsh reed and would play it when he was saddened and his heart was heavy. The image of Pan playing a flute appears often on the early city coins (See cover picture). Another statue, a fine head of a child, was found in the Palace (NO. 6).

Three other objects remind us of the extensive pagan worship at the site: two offering dishes made of glass (NOS. 113–114)

and one of clay (NO. 14). The latter was selected from hundreds left by devotees at the sanctuary and discovered during the excavations.

THE FINDS FROM THE URBAN CENTER

Most of the artifacts displayed were discovered by the Joint Expedition in the urban center of Caesarea Philippi. The majority of these date to the Middle Ages, since the excavation concentrated on uncovering the Crusader city fortress and the Ayyubid/Mamluk fortifications. Roman Banias, which lay beneath these structures, was seriously damaged by them. Later residents used earlier buildings as quarries, taking whatever materials they could find in order to fulfill their own construction needs. During the Islamic periods, for example, large amounts of marble were removed from the magnificent Roman buildings, crushed, burned,

No. 8

No. 7

Nos. 113–114

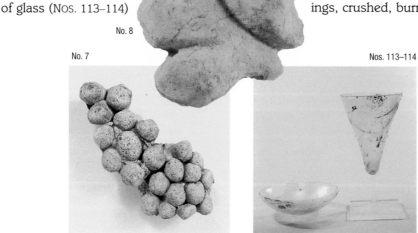

Architectural fragments and glass offering dishes

THE ARTIFACTS

and used as lime. Dozens of statues met the same fate. Despite all this, some objects survived and, as the excavation continues, others will no doubt come to light.

THE FINDS FROM THE ROMAN PERIOD

In addition to the statue fragments, the material culture of the Roman period is represented by a fig leaf that was once part of a marble decoration (No. 8), and a cluster of grapes made from stucco, once part of an architectural decoration in one of the fine Roman buildings (No. 7). Various ceramic objects represent the period as well: cooking and serving vessels, lamps, and offering vessels (Nos. 10–20). Many of these were made in local kilns and share many characteristics with pottery created at other nearby sites in Northern Israel and the

Golan. Dating from the first to the fourth centuries, these finds are contemporary with the reigns of Philip and Agrippa II (a time during which stucco was widely used) and the glorious days of Roman supremacy in the succeeding three centuries.

A fragment of a Greek inscription is etched with four letters that apparently are part of the name AGRIPPA (No. 9). While this was a relatively common name in the second and third centuries, it is entirely possible that it refers to the famous biblical king himself. Signs of the original magnificence of the Royal Palace may be seen in the fragments of splendid wall mosaics found in the basilica (throne room?) made of blue glass and colored stones and the bronze pins used to hold the marble facades that decorated the walls. Some of the latter were found *in situ* (Nos. 98–100).

No. 9

Marble fragment with inscription [A]GRIP[PA]

THE ARTIFACTS

THE FINDS FROM THE BYZANTINE PERIOD

Most of the Byzantine period finds displayed come from an important assemblage discovered in the "Street of the Shops" found in the city center in 1992. These shops were in use from the second half of the fourth century to the beginning of the fifth century C.E. The street was destroyed by a great conflagration and was apparently abandoned quite suddenly, leaving hundreds of vessels, metal objects, and coins *in situ*. The builders of the Crusader period fortifications did not know of the existence of the Byzantine street that lay only a few centimeters beneath them; thus, they were left undisturbed.

The finds from the Byzantine street include storage vessels, such as amphorae, basins, and pithoi characteristic of the northern part of the country and from the Golan, as well as tableware and servingware such as bowls, jugs, juglets, cooking vessels, and many vessels never before found intact

in excavations (NOS. 22–37). Taken together, these will enhance our knowledge of the pottery of the region and will be of great importance in further research. About thirty lamps of the "northern type" (NOS. 40–41) were found. These had been known hitherto primarily only from the excavation of tombs in the northern part of the country. Some of the lamps are decorated and others are not. Alongside the pottery vessels were found bronze and gold jewelry (NOS. 81–89), a metal balance scale (NO. 101), glass vessels (NOS. 115–117), glass windows, and coins, the latest of which is dated 408 C.E. These finds lead to the assumption that the Street of the Shops was not in use after the first quarter of the fifth century or, at the very latest, the middle of the fifth century C.E.

Other finds from the Byzantine period consist of decorated bone objects, among which are handles (NOS. 64–65), spindle whorls (NOS. 72–75)

No. 70

Bone cross

Nos. 40–41

Nos. 25–26

Nos. 22–24

Ceramic objects

THE ARTIFACTS

Medieval slip-painted bowl (No. 45)

and combs (NOS. 68–69) found in Byzantine strata in various excavation areas on the site, particularly in the area of the public bathhouse. The Christian presence is reflected in a small vessel that was found in the Street of the Shops—a pilgrim flask (NO. 21) used by Christian pilgrims to carry such precious liquids as myrrh or sacred oil obtained at holy sites. This reminds us of Banias' reputation as a place of pilgrimage. A tiny bone cross (NO. 70) that was part of a pendant is also evidence of the Christian tradition.

FINDS FROM THE MIDDLE AGES

Many vessels were found from the Middle Ages and a number are displayed. They may be categorized according to types of decoration, fabric, or glaze. For instance, there are vessels with a painted decoration beneath the glaze (underglazed painted ware), handmade vessels with a geometric decoration

(geometric ware) and faience vessels (frit ware). Each group of vessels was made in a different place and at a different time. In the Crusader period and slightly thereafter, vessels were imported through the coastal region from Cyprus (early thirteenth century Cypriot sgraffito ware) and from the principalities of Antioch (Port St. Symeon ware). In the Ayyubid/Mamluk periods the pottery shows a definite affinity with Syria, especially with regard to faience vessels. There were locally produced vessels and those that were produced in Syria, perhaps even in Damascus. The connection with Damascus, primarily in the thirteenth and fourteenth centuries C.E., is also mentioned in the historical sources of the time. The majority of these vessels were decorated, glazed, and at times accompanied by an Arabic inscription or an inscription-like decoration.

Nos. 32–37

Ceramics from the Byzantine "Street of Shops"

THE ARTIFACTS

THE POTTERY VESSELS

Bowls – The bowls displayed in the exhibition belong for the most part to the type treated with a wash beneath a yellow glaze (slip-painted ware). The bowls are round, conical, or carinated in shape, and they are frequently decorated with geometric patterns such as a net and irregular lines, a star (No. 43), and, on rare occasions, coils (No. 45). These patterns probably imitate imported vessels. Similar vessels have been found in Syria, Lebanon, Transjordan, Israel, Egypt, and Byzantium, dating from the twelfth to the fourteenth century C.E.

Bowls with a monochrome glaze (usually green in color) began to appear in the second half of the thirteenth century in Israel, Syria, and Lebanon. The yellow glaze was less common (No. 42). Bowls of this type continued to exist into the fourteenth century C.E. and even afterwards.

No. 57

Jugs (Nos. 51–53) – The geometric decoration first appeared on small jugs already in the Early Islamic period. In the twelfth century a group of hand-made vessels with painted decorations (geometric ware) appeared and continued being produced until the eighteenth century C.E. Similar vessels have appeared at sites in Transjordan, Syria, and Lebanon. In the first half of the thirteenth century, jugs appeared that are made from light-colored clay and have a bloated neck, spout, and a handle extending from the center of the neck to the shoulder of the vessel.

Juglets (No. 54) – Small juglets with a small neck and a spherical, ribbed body were found next to the vessel mentioned above.

Cooking Vessels – Cooking pots, cooking bowls, and numerous frying pans were found in the Crusader, Ayyubid, and Mamluk strata in Banias. The vessels come in different shapes, sizes, and glazes. The small cooking

No. 55

No. 60

No. 56

Ceramic objects from the Middle Ages

pot dating to the Crusader period (No. 55) has a dark brown and purple glaze that typifies the vessels from the Crusader period, whereas the yellowish brown or greenish brown glaze appears on vessels from the Mamluk period.

Special Vessels – A small ceramic measuring/dipping spoon (No. 57) and an animal head of a zoomorphic vessel treated with a wash beneath a yellow glaze (No. 56) were also found in medieval strata. They represent the diverse selection of vessels that was discovered in the area of the fortress and in its various buildings.

Ceramic Lamps – Many intact lamps were found. Based on the presence of soot on the nozzles, they seem to have been used.

On the other hand, an enormous number of broken lamps were found with only the saucers preserved. Some scholars believe that these lamps were deliberately broken so as to be used as candlesticks for wax candles. This change in the method of lighting probably occurred in the Ottoman period.

Examples of wheel-made lamps exhibited include unglazed "beehive" or "saucer" lamps (No. 60) that first appeared in the First Islamic period, glazed beehive lamps decorated with a wash beneath the glaze, glazed lamps with spouts (No. 50) and glazed, pinched lamps (No. 59). The majority of the types found at Banias have also been discovered at sites in Israel, Transjordan, Syria, Lebanon,

No. 50

**Medieval "frit" jug with
transparent turquoise glaze**

and Egypt, dating from the twelfth century C.E. The lamps with spouts continued to be used until the fifteenth century, and the pinched lamps continued until the Ottoman period.

Faience Vessels (NOS. 48, 50) – In the twelfth century the potters of Seljuk Persia began to produce vessels from a synthetic white material called "faience" (e.g., frit or soft paste). The vessels were made as imitations of Chinese porcelain. At first, white vessels were made that were decorated with engraving or incising. This technique quickly spread, and in the second half of the twelfth century vessels were made with an alkali glaze in different colors. In the Ayyubid and Mamluk periods, more vessels began

to appear decorated with underglaze patterns (underglaze painted ware). Many vessels of this type were found at Banias, three of which are displayed in this exhibition.

Ceramic "Pomegranates" (NOS. 61–62) – Some scholars believe these objects were used as weapons and others that they were for storing precious or dangerous liquids such as mercury. Some twenty complete or broken "pomegranates" were found at Banias within the various strata of the Crusader fortress and the Ayyubid/Mamluk fortifications. This reinforces the assumption that these vessels were some kind of incendiary weapon that exploded on impact by means of flammable material contained inside it.

No. 62

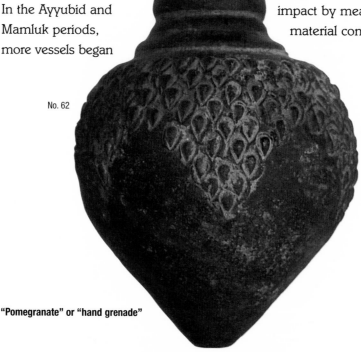

"Pomegranate" or "hand grenade"

METAL ARTIFACTS
by Elias Khamis

METAL ARTIFACTS

Various metal objects were found at Banias that range in date from the Roman period until the Late Middle Ages, some of which are presented in the exhibition. In contrast with the pottery and glass vessels, which are indicative of the cooking, eating, and drinking customs in antiquity, the metal objects tell us something about economic and social conditions. For instance, the presence of the scales and weights attests to the commercial activity in the city. The use of gold, silver, and bronze jewelry, along with cosmetic implements, attests to the cultivation of feminine beauty and reflects the fashion and aesthetic sense of women throughout the periods. The presence of these objects, and of bronze vessels alongside those of pottery and glass vessels, indicates a variety of economic and social classes in the city.

Some of the objects reveal the occupations of some of the city's populace. A fisherman's needle testifies to fishing in streams around the city. Agricultural tools such as a pruning hook and an axe attest to the occupation of farming and felling trees. The weaponry shows that, like the majority of the cities, Banias experienced periods of both peace and war. The presence of arrowheads characteristic of Crusader times hints at the unstable security situation that prevailed during that period.

Weights (Nos. 102–106) – A number of very well-preserved bronze weights dating to the Early Islamic period were found in Banias. They follow the system established at the beginning of the reign of the Umayyad caliph ʿAbd al-Malik ben Marwan (around 696 C.E.). Two units were used, the dinar and the dirham (one dirham is equal to 7/10 of a dinar). The weight of the dinar was established at 4.25 grams

No. 103

No. 106

No. 104

Islamic weights

and that of the dirham at 2.97 grams. The Byzantine division of the weight, itself primarily Roman, was, in general, accepted by the Moslems. The Byzantine *libra*, which is divided into twelve *unciae*, became the Moslem *ra* divided into twelve *wiqiyyot*. The *wiqiyya* consisted of ten dirham.

The use of lead and bronze weights is known from the classical Greek world and the Hellenistic period and continued in the Roman and Byzantine periods. One of the most common shapes of the Roman weight is the "barrel weight" made from bronze. This shape weight continued to exist until the Late Roman period and the beginning of the Byzantine period. Later these weights began to disappear, and their place was taken by square-shaped weights or discus weights. In the Fatimid period (or prior to it) the classical barrel weight again appeared in a slightly altered form.

A number of weights in the dirham series are presented in the exhibition. These weights were issued in a series of one hundred, fifty, twenty, ten, five, two, and one dirham. The smaller weights weigh a half, third, and quarter dirham. The large weights in the series are usually barrel shaped, and the smaller are square, rectangular, and sometimes cube shaped. Occasionally there are exceptions. The technique by which these weights were made is not sufficiently clear; however, they were probably cast and finished by hand. The signs of the finishing

No. 109

Medieval bronze jug

process can clearly be seen following the adjustment for the exact weight, after which the weights were decorated and struck with the official stamps.

Cosmetic Implements (NOS. 96–97) – A number of cosmetic implements were found in the Banias excavations; most were used as small spoons and some were used as cosmetic applicators. The most common cosmetic spoon in the classical periods is the spatula, with an elongated small spoon shaped like a leaf. In contrast, cosmetic spoons from the Early Islamic period have a small spoon in the shape of a small round bowl. These spatulae and the rest of the cosmetic implements from the Roman and Byzantine periods were usually decorated with a pattern of reeds and beads in the area where the stick meets the spoon. This decoration was probably made on a lathe. On the other

hand, a similar decoration of reeds and beads on cosmetic spoons and sticks from the Early Islamic period was made by means of filing, which produced a more schematic pattern. Another schematic pattern that is characteristic of the cosmetic implements from the Early Islamic period is a floral decoration stamped on the flat part created between the stick and the spoon.

Cosmetic applicators were found alongside the spoons. These applicators are characterized by the two ends that are usually smooth and curved. On the majority of the applicators known to us from scholarly publications, there is a decoration in the center of the stick. This decoration is apparently provided in order to facilitate the holding of the implement, preventing its sliding or slipping between the fingers.

No. 84

Nos. 90–91

No. 86

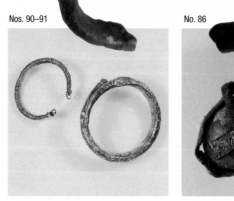

Islamic and Byzantine jewelry: ring, bracelets, pendant

METAL ARTIFACTS

Jewelry (Nos. 81–93) – Jewelry was found in Banias dating from the Byzantine period to the Middle Ages. This jewelry was made from gold, silver, and bronze and included bracelets, pendants, rings, and buckles. The gold and silver jewelry were made by trained goldsmiths who learned their craft in the urban centers and created jewelry in keeping with the fashion that prevailed in the same period. Bronze or iron jewelry, on the other hand, was made by metal craftsmen who did not usually invest a lot of effort in designing the jewelry they produced. The life span of a form of jewelry made from inexpensive metal can extend for hundreds of years. It is therefore difficult to date these types based on comparisons with finds from excavations or collections.

Arrowheads (Nos. 107–108) – Arrowheads and spearheads made from iron were found in the Banias excavations. All have a typical tang

that is round in section. This tang was inserted into a reed and was fixed in place by means of string that was bound around the end of it. Iron arrowheads and spearheads that have an elongated pyramid shape and a tri-angular section first appeared in the Roman period. The use of this type probably continued in our region until the Early Islamic period. The iron arrowhead with an elongated pyramid shape and a square section appar-ently replaced that which was triangular in section during the Early Islamic period. Its use continued into the Crusader and Mamluk periods.

No. 107

No. 108

Spear and arrowhead

METAL ARTIFACTS

Bronze Pins for Fastening Marble
(NOS. 98–100) – Together with the use of marble came the use of bronze pegs whose function was to fix the marble slabs along the height of the walls of the magnificent buildings. These pegs were usually made from relatively thick, broad strips of bronze. One of their ends was bent at a right angle and was bifurcated and inserted into a hole in the wall that was prepared in advance. This hole was later sealed with a lump of lead that fastened the peg to the wall. The other end of the peg is thinner, and it too was bent perpendicular and was used to anchor the marble slab to the wall. The use of bronze rather than iron for making these pegs prevented the marble from slipping out over the years, since, unlike iron, they did not swell, rust, and disintegrate.

Bronze Vessels – The bronze vessels exhibited are dated to the Middle Ages (Mamluk period), based on their shape and the archaeological context in which they were found. Bronze vessels are considered a rare find in an excavation. The majority of these vessels were made by means of hammering a thin sheet of copper. The corrosion process, acting on the delicate vessels for hundreds of years while buried in the soil, caused their disintegration and disappearance. What sometimes remains from the bronze vessels are the handles, the feet made in a casting, and occasionally the rim or base. Because these bronze vessels are dated to relatively late periods, the corrosive process was not completed and its damage to the vessels was relatively minor.

No. 98   No. 99   No.100

Bronze pins for fastening marble

GLASS OBJECTS

by Yael Gorin-Rosen

GLASS OBJECTS

Excavations within the early city of Caesarea Philippi (Banias) and the medieval fort and fortifications yielded a large number of glass vessels and other glass objects, such as beads, pendants, glass inlays, windowpanes, fragments of glass tiles, and glass tesserae. Only a few of these were found complete or could be restored.

The glass vessels represent a long time span, from the Late Hellenistic period up to the recent century (the Syrian village). The majority of the finds date from the Roman period (primarily the late Roman city); the Byzantine city, and the Islamic period (primarily in its later stages). They reflect all aspects of daily life through tablewares, luxurious vessels, cosmetics, and religious items, and also as part of the architecture.

Remains of an extensive glass workshop were found at the site, contemporary with the Crusader and Ayyubid/Mamluk fortifications. This workshop probably continued an earlier tradition of glass production in the city of Banias, originating in the Roman or Byzantine periods. The finds that identified this workshop are mainly raw glass chunks in various colors and glass industry wasters (NO. 123). The glass is mainly colorless with yellow and green tinges, or of purple hues. These colors characterized the Late Islamic and Medieval vessels, as opposed to bluish-green glass that characterized the Roman and Byzantine periods. Three assemblages of glass objects are represented in the exhibition.

No. 123

Raw glass for the production of glass vessels:
Crusader and Ayyubid/Mamluk periods

GLASS OBJECTS

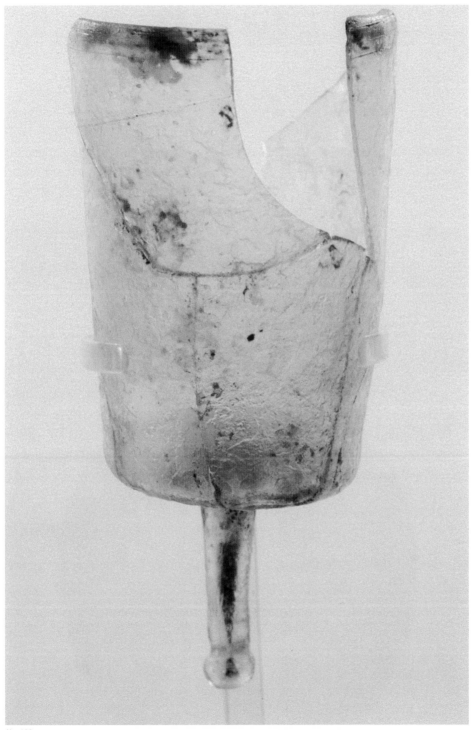

No. 122

Hanging oil lamp made of glass

GLASS OBJECTS

Finds from the Sanctuary of Pan (NOS. 113–114) – The first assemblage was found at the Sanctuary of Pan, consisting primarily of bowls and beakers that were probably used as ceremonial vessels in the sanctuary. It is one of the best-preserved glass assemblages connected to a religious site found to date.

Finds from the Byzantine "Street of Shops" – The second group, dated to the Roman period, was found in the earlier phase of the burned-out shops (NOS. 115–117). It includes a group of Roman vessels, such as an Aryballos dated probably to the third century C.E. and a deformed conical beaker with blue blobs as decoration, dated to the fourth century C.E.

The Islamic Periods – The third group assemblage consists of glass vessels from various Islamic periods, including perfume bottles of different shapes and sizes (NOS. 118–120) and a glass oil lamp (NO. 122). Perfume bottles were popular throughout all Islamic periods and were made in various shapes and decorated in different techniques. Glass oil lamps were widely used from the Byzantine period until the Industrial Revolution. They were common everywhere during the Islamic period.

No. 121

Glass pilgrim flask

THE COINS
by John F. Wilson

THE COINS

Coins were minted at Banias for more than two centuries, beginning with the reign of Philip, son of Herod the Great (4 B.C.E.–34 C.E.). Philip's coins featured the temple at Banias erected in honor of the Roman Emperor Augustus (NO. 124). The first issue of his grandson, Agrippa II, dates to the time of the Jewish War (64–70 C.E.), temporarily renaming the city Neronias in honor of the Emperor Nero (NO. 125). Later, Agrippa II minted many Roman-style coins at Banias, some of which celebrated the Roman victory over Agrippa's fellow Jews by depicting the goddess Nike (NO. 128). His name clearly appears on coins minted during the time the palace was being constructed

(NOS. 126 and 127). Coins of the second and third centuries illustrate Banias' function as a pagan religious site. They describe the city as "Caesarea Sebastos (Augustus), holy and city of refuge, which stands before the sanctuary of Pan." The gods most commonly appearing on the coins are Pan himself (NO. 130); his father or grandfather, Zeus (NO. 129); and Tyche ("Lady Luck"), the patroness of the city's prosperity (NO.131). The city's symbols were a short crooked club (called a pedum or a "rabbit thumper," used by shepherds to kill small animals) and a syrinx—the famous "pipes of Pan" with which the goat god beguiled the nymphs of the forest (NO.132).

No. 127
No. 126
No. 129
No. 132
No. 124
No. 131
No. 125
No. 128
No. 130

THE CATALOG

THE CATALOG

STATUARY AND ARCHITECTURAL FRAGMENTS FROM ROMAN CAESAREA PHILIPPI: THE HERODIAN CITY AND PAGAN SANCTUARY

No. 1

1. Head of Athena Wearing Attic Helmet. Painted, nearly life-size head, wearing an Attic helmet, broken at the base of the neck. The head turns to the left and tilts slightly toward the side. The oval-shaped head is framed by a painted Attic helmet. For discussion see Friedland 1997: 118–122, Figs. 10–13.[1]

IAA: 2000-3248
Locus: 192
Basket: 7167-1
Height: 0.23m
Width: 0.17m
Depth: 0.22m
Material: white marble, small crystals

No. 2

2. Head of Zeus or Asclepios. Two joining fragments of a life-size bearded male head turning to the right and tilting slightly downward. The oval shape of the face is accentuated by a frame of long, doughy locks and a short, curly beard. For further discussion see Friedland 1997: 126–130, Figs. 18–21.

IAA: 2000-3249
Locus: 705
Basket 7805-1
Height: 0.26m
Width: 0.16m
Depth: 0.20m
Material: white marble; medium, glittering, flaky crystals

3. Artemis Rospigliosi (no photo). These fragments represent a two-thirds life-size statue of a draped, booted female figure running toward the right. The left leg is bent and turned outward, while the left leg is straight and extended behind the body. For further information see Friedland 1997: 173–180, Figs. 54–55.

IAA: 2000-3247-1
Locus: 702
Basket: 7767-1
Scale/Reconstructed Height: two-thirds life-size; 0.94m
Height: 0.79m
Depth: 0.34m
Material: white marble; small to medium, glittering crystals

No. 4

4. Male Head (An Emperor?). A small head carved in a highly unnaturalistic style. The oval head turns toward the left (Friedland 1997: 217–221, Fig. 80).

IAA: 2000-3330
Locus: 716
Basket: 8116-1
Height: 0.06m
Width: 0.05m
Depth: 0.05m
Material: white marble

---

[1] Elise Friedland, Roman Marble Sculpture from the Levaut: The Group from the Sanctuary of Pan at Caesarea Philippi (Paneas). Ph.D. Dissertation, University of Michigan, 1997.

THE CATALOG

5. Hand of Pan Playing the Flute. One of three Pan-related fragments found at the sanctuary. Here Pan holds a syrinx, whereas on the coins of Paneas he plays a single-reed flute. The syrinx does appear on the coins as a symbol of the city, however (see section on coins).

IAA: 2000-3329
Locus: 714
Basket: 8189-1

No. 5

No. 6

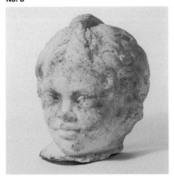

6. Head of a Child. A life-size head of a child, whose hair is made up of a braid in the middle of the head from the forehead toward the back. The sides are made of a group of curls covering the rest of the head to the ears. Traces of red color are seen around the eyes and on top of the forehead.

IAA: 2000-3395
Locus: 18I001
Basket: 18I0009
Height: 0.18m
Width: 0.15m
Depth: 0.15m
Material: white marble, small crystals

7. Cluster of Grapes. An architectural decoration.

IAA: 2000-3383
Locus: 17D053
Basket: 17D0056z
Length and width: 6cm
Depth: 3.5cm.
Material: stucco

No. 7

No. 8

8. Fig Leaf. Fragment of a marble decoration.

IAA: 200-3230
Locus: 2B053
Basket 2B0259-17
Length: 7cm
Width: 8cm
Material: white marble

No. 9

10. Mosaic Fragment (no photo). Sections of a magnificent mosaic decoration were discovered in the "throne room" (apse of the basilica) of the palace. The surviving pieces of this delicately fashioned work are unfortunately too fragmentary to determine what scene was originally depicted.

9. Fragment of a marble inscription ("Agrippa"?). Fragment of marble inscription incised with four Greek letters, which translate to GRIP, probably to be completed [A]GRIP[PA] ("Agrippa"). Quite possibly part of an inscription mentioning King Agrippa II of Banias, the grandson of Herod the Great.

IAA: 2000-3229
Locus: 1A003
Basket: 1A0036j
Length: 13cm
Width: 7cm

CERAMICS FROM ROMAN CAESAREA PHILIPPI: THE HERODIAN CITY AND PAGAN SANCTUARY

Nos. 11–12

11. Roman Oil Lamp, Non-Decorated "Disk" Type

IAA: 2000-3358
Locus: 13D002
Basket: 13D0039n

12. Roman Oil Lamp, Decorated "Disk" Type

IAA: 2000-3361
Locus: 13D002
Basket: 13D0040-3n

THE CATALOG

No. 13

13. Woman's Head on Clay. Head of a woman, probably originally the decoration on the discus of a Roman oil lamp.

IAA: 2000-3392:
Locus: 18D006
Basket: 18D0222
Length and width: 2cm

No. 14

14. Offering Bowl. Hundreds of these locally produced bowls or "saucer lamps," dating from the second to the fourth centuries, were found at the area of the Sanctuary of Pan where they had been left by worshippers. This bowl was found within the complex of the Roman palace.

IAA: 2000-3394
Locus: 18D069
Basket: 18D0418
Length: 3cm
Diameter: 9.5cm
Base diameter: 4.5cm

Nos. 15–20

15–20. 2ND–4TH CENTURY POTTERY

15. Banias Bowl

IAA: 2000-3327
Locus: 11D009
Basket 11D0049

18. Small Cooking Pot

IAA: 2000-3339
Locus 12D016
Basket: 12D0193

16. Carinated Bowl

IAA: 2000-3364
Locus: 14I003
Basket: 14I0024-1

19. Small Cooking Pot

IAA: 2000-3340
Locus: 12D016
Basket 12D0156-2

17. Jug

IAA: 2000-3345
Locus: 12D006
Basket: 12D0192

20. Dipping Juglet

IAA: 2000-3344
Locus: 12I015
Basket: 12I0090-1

THE CATALOG

OBJECTS FROM BYZANTINE PANEAS: THE CHRISTIAN CITY

All of the following vessels were found in the "Street of Shops" and are dated from the second half of the fourth century up to the beginning of the fifth century.

No. 21

21. **Pilgrim's Flask.** Small ampula with two loop handles and incised geometric decoration, used by pilgrims to carry precious liquids such as myrrh or sacred oil from holy places.

IAA: 2000-3302
Locus: 8F008
Basket: SF0159
Length: 8cm
Width: 5.5cm
Depth: 3 cm
(Photo 73)

Nos. 22–24

22–24. PLATES AND BOWLS

22. Large Plate

IAA: 2000-3293
Locus: 8F014
Basket: 8F0183

23. Platter

IAA: 2000-3294
Locus: 8F005
Basket: 8F0014

24. Carinated Bowl

IAA: 2000-3295
Locus: 8F008
Basket: 8F0087

Nos. 25–26

25–26. STORAGE VESSELS

25. Wine Amphora

IAA: 2000-3297
Locus: 8F008
Basket: 8F0106

26. Wine Amphora

IAA: 20003296
Locus: 8F009
Basket: 8F0107

THE CATALOG

27–31. JUGS, JUGLETS, FLASK, AND AMPHORISCUS

27. Flask-Jug with Pine Tree Decoration

IAA: 2000-3289
Locus: 8F008
Basket: 8F0090

28. Flask-Jug

IAA: 2000-3251
Locus: 8F008
Basket: 80039

29. Jug

IAA: 2000-3250
Locus: 8F008
Basket: 8F0071

30. Juglet

IAA: 2000-3643
Locus: 8F014
Basket: 8F0258

31. Amphoriscus

IAA: 2000-3283
Locus: 8F008
Basket: 8F0043

Nos. 27–31

Nos. 32–37

32–37. JUGS, JUGLETS, BUTTER CHURN, AND COOKING POT

32. Jug

IAA: 2000-3252
Locus: 8F008
Basket: 8F0062

33. Jug

IAA: 2000-3282
Locus: 8F008
Basket: 8F0086

34. Butter Churn

IAA 2000-3290
Locus 8F008
Basket 8F0050

35. Dipping Juglet

IAA: 2000-3286
Locus: 8F008
Basket: 8F0038

36. Dipping Juglet

IAA: 2000-3287
Locus: 8F008
Basket: 8F0103

37. Small Cooking Pot

IAA: 2000-3288
Locus: 8F011
Basket: 8F0257

Nos. 38–39

38–39. LIDS (Probably Lantern Lids)

38. Lid

IAA: 2000-3298
Locus: 8F008
Basket: 8F0127-2

39. Lid

IAA: 2000-3299
Locus: 8F008
Basket: 8F0127-1

Nos. 40–41

40–41. LATE ROMAN-BYZANTINE "NORTHERN" OIL LAMPS.
These lamps are designated "northern lamps" because they are a common type from this period found in the northern part of Israel during the late Roman and Byzantine periods.

40. Lamp

IAA: 2000-3301
Locus: 8F008
Basket: 8F0142

41. Lamp

IAA: 2000-3300
Locus: 8F008
Basket: 8F0146

THE CATALOG

CERAMICS FROM MEDIEVAL BANIAS: FROM FORTRESS TO ISLAMIC VILLAGE

No. 42

42. Monochrome Yellow Glazed Bowl. A bowl with a simple rim and high ring base, made of orange-brown clay, and decorated with a white slip and yellow glaze, dated from the second half of the thirteenth century to the fourteenth century.

IAA: 2000-3375
Locus: 14I011
Basket: 14I0088
Height: 7cm
Rim Diameter: 16cm
Base Diameter: 6cm

Nos. 43–44

43–44. Slip-painted Bowls: Twelfth–Fourteenth Centuries. Rounded, conical, or carinated bowls with yellow or green glaze started to appear at the eleventh century C.E. and became particularly popular during the Mamluk period.

43. Slip-painted Bowl with Star Pattern

IAA: 2000-3376
Locus: 14I036
Basket: 14I0225
Height: 7.5cm
Rim Diameter: 23cm
Base Diameter: 9cm

44. Slip-painted Bowl with Geometric Patterns of Net and Irregular Lines

IAA: 2000-3692
Locus: 5B999
Basket: 5B1492
Height: 8.5cm
Rim Diameter: 20.5cm
Base Diameter: 8cm

No. 45

45. Large Slip-painted Bowl. Large bowl decorated with coils. This pattern is quite rare, imitating imported vessels.

Locus: 13I016
Basket: 13I0105
Height: 10cm
Rim Diameter: 34cm
Base Diameter: 12cm

46. Slip-painted Saucer Lamp

IAA: 2000-3341
Locus: 12I011
Basket: 12I0056

47. Islamic Lamp

IAA: 2000-3378
Locus: 14I011
Basket: 14I0116

No. 48

48. "Frit" Underglaze Painted Bowl. A conic bowl with high ring base made of white faience and covered with transparent alkaline glaze. Blue decoration appears beneath a clear turquoise glaze. This bowl, as well as all other vessels of this type found in Israel, was apparently made in Syria at the end of the twelfth century C.E. These vessels are also known from Persia and Egypt in the thirteenth century C.E.

IAA: 2000-3309
Locus: 8G004
Basket: 8G0053
Height: 8cm
Rim Diameter: 17cm
Base Diameter: 6cm

49. Neck of Large "Frit" Jar. In the second half of the thirteenth century, vessels with a blue and black decoration under a colorless, transparent alkaline glaze began to appear. This neck of a very large jar belonging to this family of vessels is decorated with geometric patterns. The jug was apparently made in a Damascus workshop.

IAA: 2000-3335
Locus: 12B011
Basket: 12B0048

No. 50

50. "Frit" Jug with Transparent Turquoise Glaze. A unique jug made of frit/faience with ledge rim, smoothed neck, broad body above and narrow below, decorated with vertical lines fashioned in relief (probably in a mold). Three small vertical handles adorn the shoulders of the vessel, which is glazed with a transparent turquoise alkaline glaze.

IAA: 2000-3379
Locus: 14I036
Basket: 14I0227-1
Height: 25cm
Rim Diameter: 10.5 cm
Base Diameter: 10cm

Nos. 51–53

51–53. JUGS. "Geometric ware" vessels were manufactured in various sizes from the end of the twelfth century to the end of the Mamluk period. These were made of light-brown clay, mixed with straw, and were poorly fired. The vessels were covered with white, light brown, light red, or an orange slip and burnished. The surface was decorated with geometric designs in red, brown, or purple. Many jugs of this type were uncovered in Banias. Simple jugs made of light orange-brown clay started to appear at the thirteenth century. These are characterized by a blown neck, spout, and handle.

51. "Geometric ware" Jug

IAA: 2000-3333
Locus: 12D024
Basket: 12D0211

53. Simple Brown-Necked Jug

IAA: 2000-3331
Locus: 12I004
Basket: 12I0007

52. Small "Geometric ware" Jug

IAA: 2000-3236
Locus: 6C999;
Basket: 6C0549

THE CATALOG

54. Juglet

IAA: 2000-3380
Locus: 14I003
Basket: 14I0048
Height: 8cm
Rim and Base Diameter: 4.5cm

No. 55

55. Small Crusader Period Cooking Pot. No neck, simple rim, two horizontal handles, purple glaze inside.

IAA: 2000-3322
Locus: 10B039
Basket: 10B0109

No. 56

56. Zoomorphic Slip-painted Head. Head of an animal probably once decorating a vessel.

IAA: 2000-3349
Locus: 13D012
Basket: 13D0132zp

THE CATALOG

No. 57

57. Dipping Spoon

IAA: 2000-3368
Locus: 14I010
Basket: 14I0129zp
Length: 12.5cm
Width: 5.5cm
Base Diameter: 4cm

No. 58

58. Glazed, Spouted Oil Lamp. Made in the form of a small juglet with a spout and handle of reddish-brown clay, spots of white slip, and green glaze. May be dated to the Mamluk period (twelfth to fifteenth centuries).

IAA: 2000-3237
Locus: 6C151
Basket: 6C0638

No. 59

59. Pinched, Green-glazed Lamp. Featuring a small bowl with flat base and pinched rim, this type is dated from the thirteenth century up to the Ottoman period.

IAA: 2000-3310
Locus: 8B016
Basket: 8B0126

60. Non-glazed "Beehive" or "Saucer" Lamp. This type of lamp is made of two bowls; the bigger one serves as a base with pinched rim; the small bowl is put upside down on top of it and is used as a place for the oil. It has a broad filling hole and a handle. Dated twelfth–thirteenth centuries.

IAA: 2000-3342
Locus: 12D035
Basket: 12D0301

No. 60

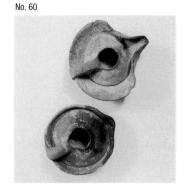

Nos. 61–62

61–62. "HAND GRENADES." Two principle types of these carefully decorated objects are found: green and purple/mauve. They were probably used as "grenades," exploding on impact. Some scholars believe, however, that they were used for storing mercury. (In the excavations at Beth Shean, evidence of mercury was found inside a vessel of this type.)

61. Purple Type

IAA: 2000-3228
Locus: 1A999
Basket: 1A0182
Height: 11cm
Width: 8cm

62. Green Type

IAA: 2000-3233
Locus: 4C999
Basket: 4C0312-1
Height: 13.5cm
Width: 12.5cm

No. 63

63. Smoking Pipe. Many such clay pipes, with various decorations, were found at Banias, indicating the introduction of tobacco into the Ottoman Empire by European travelers and merchants in the early seventeenth century.

IAA: 2000-3388
Locus: 17K999
Basket: 17K0004e

THE CATALOG

BONE OBJECTS: VARIOUS PERIODS

No. 64

64. Incised Bone Object

IAA: 2000-3231
Locus: 3C044
Basket: 3C0190
Length: 9cm
Width: 3cm

No. 65

65. Decorated Bone Object. Probably a handle or casing for an unknown artifact.

IAA: 2000-3366
Locus: 14D010
Basket: 14D0090zb

No. 66

66. Bone Stick, Decorated with Incised Circles and Dots

IAA: 2000-3377
Locus: 14D028
Basket:14D0101zb
Length: 10cm
Width: 1cm
Depth: 0.7cm

No. 67

67. Gaming Piece

IAA: 2000-3321
Locus: 9G001
Basket: 9G0010z
Length: 4cm
Width: 2cm

Nos. 68–69

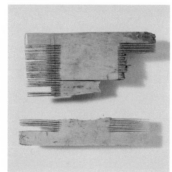

68–69. COMBS MADE OF BONE

#### 68. Comb	#### 69. Comb
IAA: 2000-3318	IAA: 2000-3319
Locus: 3C004	Locus: 8G003
Basket: 3C0030zb	Basket 8G0005zb
Length: 8cm	Length: 8cm
Width: 4cm	Width: 2cmcm

No. 70

70. Decorated Cross Made of Bone

IAA: 2000-3308
Locus: 8D005
Basket: 8D0066z

71. Amulet. This triangular-shaped object made of stone is inscribed with a number of names in Greek, including Amos and Michael. It probably served as a sort of good luck charm.

IAA: 2000-3384
Locus: 17D056
Basket: 17D0144z

No. 71

Nos. 72–75

72–75. Decorated Spindle Whorls. Spindle whorls were used in the manufacture of textiles and are found with a variety of decorations.

72. Spindle Whorl

IAA: 2000-3323
Locus: 11D009
Basket: 11D0038z

74. Spindle Whorl

IAA: 2000-3337
Locus: 12K004
Basket: 12K0023z

73. Spindle Whorl

IAA: 2000-3338
Locus: 12K003
Basket: 12K0007z

75. Spindle Whorl

IAA: 2000-3336
Locus: 12I024
Basket: 12I0230z

76. Glass Spindle Whorl
IAA: 2000-3303
Locus: 8F008
Basket: 8F0129-1z

No. 76

THE CATALOG

JEWELRY, COSMETICS, AND METAL OBJECTS: VARIOUS PERIODS

Nos. 77–80

77–80. BEADS

77. Irregular Amber Bead

IAA: 2000-3325
Locus: 11D004
Basket: 11D0003z

78. Round Amber Bead with White Lines

IAA: 2000-3324
Locus: 11H033
Basket: 11H0100z

79. Small Blue Bead

IAA: 2000-3317
Locus: 8C002
Basket: 8C0011z

80. Double Blue Bead

IAA: 2000-3316
Locus: 8G010
Basket: 8G0079z

No. 83

81. Wedding Ring. Judging from its size, the ring is masculine and was probably used as a wedding band.

IAA: 2000-3239
Locus: 7C999
Basket: 7C1326m
Diameter: 2.20cm
Width: 0.40cm
Thickness: 0.20cm

82. Bronze Ring with Turquoise Inlay

IAA: 2000-3234
Locus: 5B244
Basket: 5B1398
Height: 2.10cm
Thickness: 0.10cm

83. Bronze Finger Ring with Lion. Preserved on the frame is a decoration in sunken relief portraying a lion striding off toward the right side with its tail raised above its back. Above the lion are a star and a crescent. By means of its shape the ring is dated to the Byzantine period or the beginning of the early Islamic period.

IAA: 2000-3387
Locus: 17D081
Basket: 17D0425z
Diameter: 2.35cm
Width: 0.60cm

THE CATALOG

No. 84

84. Bronze Finger Ring with Pseudo-Arabic Inscription. A cast-bronze finger ring with a small rectangular plate on which are incised five identical rows of Kufic script. The ring is dated to the early Islamic period based on its shape and the engraving, which attest to its use as a seal ring. According to Moslem tradition, a seal ring is the only jewelry that males are permitted to have, and these may not be made from gold or silver that exceeds two dirham in weight.

IAA: 2000-3245
Locus: 7C160
Basket: 7C1277
Diameter: 2.40cm
Thickness: 0.25cm
Rectangular part: 1.20 x 1.50cm

No. 84

No. 85

85. Metal Pendant with Cross of Incised Circles. A triangular-shaped bronze pendant. On the inner side of the triangle is a cross-shaped decoration composed of five small circles stamped onto each arm.

IAA: 2000-3241
Locus: 3C130
Basket: 3C0613m
Length: 4.90cm
Width: 3.00cm
Thickness: 0.20cm

No. 86

86. Metal Pendant Frame with Glass "Stone." This pendant consists of a small oval lump of transparent glass—apparently an inexpensive imitation of a semiprecious stone, such as rock crystal. The lump of glass is bound by two thin, broad strips of bronze. These strips were joined in their center by a bronze wire. It was found in the so-called "Street of Shops."

IAA: 2000-3304
Locus: 8F008
Basket: 8F0158
Length: 3.40cm
Width: 1.70cm

THE CATALOG

87–89. GOLD JEWELRY FROM THE "STREET OF SHOPS." A hollow central cylinder surrounded by three smaller cylinders. The cylinders are tapered close toward the top to ensure a better grip on the stones inlaid into each one of them. Between the three small cylinders are two even smaller cylinders, one of which is inlaid with a light-colored stone. The stones in the rest of the cylinders are lost. The ornament is partially crushed; however, its overall shape was almost completely preserved. The shape, technique, and context in which it was found date it to the Byzantine period. The gold pendant is inlaid with a black stone. The stone itself is inlaid with gold wire in the shape of a cross or flower with four petals. This pendant probably served as an inlay for the ornament described above. The loop was used for suspending some sort of gold ornament, such as an earring or pendant.

Nos. 87–89

Nos. 90–91

No. 92

87. Gold Earring or Medallion

IAA: 2000-3386
Locus: 8F005
Basket: 8F0019/1
Length: 2.00cm
Width: 2.00cm
Height: 0.80cm
Thickness: 0.05cm

88. Heart-shaped Pendant

IAA: 2000-3386
Locus: 8F005
Basket: 8F0019/2.
Length: 0.80cm
Width: 0.70cm
Thickness: 0.20cm

89. Gold Loop

IAA: 2000-3386
Locus: 17D081
Basket: 17D04752.
Diameter: 1.30cm
Thickness: 0.10cm

90–91. DECORATED SILVER BRACELETS. Composed of hollow, beaten-silver plate, these bracelets are similar to others dating to the Fatimid period found in various excavations in the country.

90. Silver Bracelet

IAA: 2000-3390
Locus: 18D001
Basket: 18D0023/1
Diameter: 8.70cm
Thickness: 1.45cm

91. Silver Bracelet

IAA: 2000-3391
Locus: 18D001
Basket: 18D0023/2
Diameter: 6.60cm
Thickness: 0.80cm

92. Bronze Bracelet

IAA: 2000-3305
Locus: 8F008
Basket: 8F0088m
Diameter: 7.30cm
Maximum Thickness: 0.35cm

93. Bronze Bracelet. A broken bronze bracelet consisting of four bronze wires twisted around in the form of a braid. Similar bracelets found in other excavations range in date from the Hellenistic period until the Crusader period and even later.

IAA: 2000-3315
Locus: 8C151
Basket: 8C0401
Diameter: 6.30cm
Thickness: 0.60cm

94. Bronze Buckle. Similar buckles have been found elsewhere dating from the Crusader period.

IAA: 2000-3240/1
Locus: 7C999
Basket: 7C0128
Length: 2.80cm
Width: 3.10cm
Thickness: 0.60cm

95. Bronze Buckle. The shape of this buckle is characteristic to the Middle Ages.

IAA: 2000-3240/2
Locus: 7C999
Basket: 7C0128
Length: 1.80cm
Width: 3.20cm
Thickness: 0.30cm

98–100. PINS FOR ATTACHING MARBLE TO WALLS. These bronze pins or pegs were used to fasten marble facing slabs to stone walls. Several such pins were found *in situ* in the palace/bath house of Banias.

98. Bronze Pin

IAA: 2000-3381/1
Locus: 14D024
Basket: 14D0104/1
Length: 12.80 cm
Width: 1.10 cm

100. Bronze Pin

IAA: 2000-3328
Locus: 11I004
Basket: 11I0056m
Length: 9.70 cm
Width: 1.60 cm

99. Bronze Pin

IAA: 2000-3381/2
Locus: 14D024
Basket: 14D0104/2
Length: 12.30 cm
Width: 0.90 cm

Nos. 96–97

Nos. 98–100

96. Bronze Cosmetic Spoon. On the flat part of the implement, between the handle and the spoon, is a decoration composed of a schematic floral lattice.

IAA: 2000-3342
Locus: 7C165
Basket: 7C1457/2
Length: 14.40cm
Width of Spoon: 0.90cm
Thickness of Stick: 0.40cm

97. Cosmetic Applicator. A decoration consisting of two beads between three reeds appears in the center of the implement in the place where it is held—apparently in order to facilitate grasping it. Because in the Roman times the cosmetic applicators were more delicate, this one should be dated to the Byzantine period.

IAA: 2000-3349
Locus: 12D012
Basket: 12D0209m
Length: 15.30 cm
Thickness: 0.60 cm

THE CATALOG

No. 101

101. Balance Scale. This bronze balance scale from the Byzantine period was found without the pans and the weights. The pans of the scales were meant to be hung from three bronze or iron chains attached to rings. On the upper surface of one of the arms are eleven equidistant grooves. On this type of scale a balance weight was hung on this side and could be slid the length of the arm. It is very probable that each one of these grooves designated an ounce.

This kind of balance scale is known from the Roman period onward and is sometimes called a "steelyard scale." It saved the merchant from using a relatively large number of weights and allowed quicker and easier weighing than ordinary scales. The measurement of the weight being used, together with the number marked on the arm by the sliding balance weight, provided the exact weight of the commodity.

IAA: 2000-3307
Locus: 8F008
Basket: 8F0055z
Length: 33.00 cm

No. 102

102. Bronze Barrel Weight. The weight is ten *waqiyyot,* which is identical to the theoretical weight of one hundred dirham. Bronze weights of this type dating to the Islamic period are usually found in smaller units, and this size is considered rare.

IAA: 2000-3393
Locus: 18D054
Basket: 18D0123m
Diameter: 4.35 cm
Height: 3.10 cm
Weight: 300 grams
Unit of weight: dirham

THE CATALOG

103–106. BRONZE WEIGHTS

103. Decorated Bronze Barrel Weight. A bronze weight decorated in the shape of a barrel with two round, flat bases. The sides of the weight are fashioned from five ground rows, each of them composed of a number of small hexagonal surfaces. The sides of the hexagon merge with the rest of the sides of the hexagonal surfaces around them, producing a pattern similar to that of a beehive. A small circle with a dot in its center is stamped on each of the hexagonal surfaces. This decoration is referred to as a "bird's eye," and it is characteristic of the weights from the early Islamic period. It was used as a twenty dirham weight—the equivalent to two *waqiyyot*.

IAA: 2000-3385
Locus: 17D023
Basket: 17D0045
Maximum diameter: 2.40 cm
Height: 1.85 cm
Weight: 57.70 grams
Unit of weight: dirham

Nos. 103–104

Nos. 106

104. Decorated Bronze Barrel Weight. The decoration of this weight is similar to the one described above. The weight is ten dirham, or one *waqiyya*.

IAA: 2000-3244
Locus: 7C999
Basket: 7C1026/2
Maximum diameter: 2.00 cm
Height 1.65 cm
Weight: 29.00 grams
Unit of weight: dirham

105. Ribbed Bronze Barrel Weight. A barrel-shaped weight in the form of two truncated, octagonal cones attached to each other at the bases. Thus, the sides consist of sixteen small trapezoid surfaces. These surfaces were produced by filing the sides of the weight, which were originally smooth. The weight has two octagonal bases, one of which is decorated with two concentric circles in the center, to which a bit of metal has been added to supplement the weight that was lacking when the weight was being crafted. The weight is ten dirham.

IAA: 2000-3246
Locus: 7C159
Basket: 7C1477
Maximum diameter: 2.15 cm
Height 1.35 cm
Weight: 29.43 grams
Unit of weight: dirham

106. Square Bronze Weight. A square bronze weight with traces of a circular stamping on the two bases. The weight is two dirham.

IAA: 2000-3243
Locus: 7C999
Basket: 7C1026/1
Length: 1.20 cm
Width: 1.10 cm
Thickness: 0.55 cm
Weight: 5.70 grams
Unit of weight: dirham

THE CATALOG

Nos. 107–108

107. Iron Spearhead. A flat, elongated spearhead made from iron in the shape of a flat leaf terminating in a sharp triangle tip.

IAA: 2000-3313
Locus: 8B004
Basket: 8B0023
Length: 12.70 cm

108. Iron Arrowhead

IAA: 2000-3314
Locus: 8B007
Basket: 8B0031z
Length: 9.70 cm

No. 109

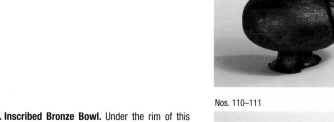

109. Bronze Jug. A bronze jug cast from a number of parts and with a shape characteristic of the Mamluk period.

IAA: 2000-3348
Locus: 12D033
Basket: 12D0290
Height: 14.40 cm
Body diameter: 13.30 cm
Rim diameter: 7.70
Width of rim: 0.50 cm

110. Inscribed Bronze Bowl. Under the rim of this bowl is a relatively large strip with an inscription in the Naschi Arabic alphabet. Bowls of this type bearing inscriptions in Naschi were well known in the Islamic world of the Middle Ages, especially in the Mamluk period.

IAA: 2000-3347
Locus: 12D014
Basket: 12D0127

111. Decorated Bronze Bowl. The bottom part of this bowl is decorated with a rosette or arcade pattern with thirteen arches, each apparently containing a decoration.

IAA: 2000-3389
Locus: 18D036
Basket: 18D0307
Rim diameter: 10.55 cm
Height: 4.30 cm

Nos. 110–111

THE CATALOG

112. **Fisherman's Netting Needle.** Only half of the needle was preserved. This type of needle was common all over the ancient world and has been found in many places. Fishermen have used such needles to make and repair their nets for a long period of history, dating back to the XII Dynasty in Egypt.

IAA: 3382
Locus: 15K001
Basket: 15K0010m
Length: 7.70 cm
Length of prong: 2.50 cm
Thickness: 0.40 cm

Nos. 113–114

GLASS OBJECTS: VARIOUS PERIODS

113–114. OFFERING VESSELS FROM THE SANCTUARY OF PAN. These vessels probably date to the fourth century C.E. and were used in connection with worship at the Sanctuary of Pan.

113. Conical Beaker

IAA: 2000-3406
Locus: 709
Basket: 7864
Rim Diameter: 10.6 cm
Height: 13.6 cm

114. Segmental Bowl

IAA: 2000-3407
Locus: 720
Basket: 8167
Rim Diameter: 14.1 cm

Nos. 115–117

115–117. GLASS VESSELS FROM THE BURNED "STREET OF SHOPS"

115. **Aryballos.** 2nd–3rd Century C.E.

IAA: 2000-3425
Locus: 8F008
Basket 8F0232
Rim Diameter: 3.8 cm
Height: c. 6 cm

116. **Small Bottle.** 2nd–3rd Century C.E.

IAA: 2000-3426
Locus: 8F008
Basket: 8F0136
Rim Diameter: 3.7 cm
Height: 11.2 cm

117. **Conical Beaker.** Probably 4th Century C.E.

IAA: 2000-3427
Locus: 8F008
Basket: 8F0079
Rim Diameter: c. 9.5 cm

THE CATALOG

118–120. SMALL MEDIEVAL PERIOD BOTTLES

118. Small Bottle.
Probably Abbasid
Period (9th–10th
centuries C.E.).

IAA: 2000-3412
Locus: 15K001
Basket: 15K0037
Rim Diameter: 1.4 cm
Height: 7.3 cm

120. Molar Flask.
9th–10th
centuries C.E.

IAA: 2000-3409
Locus: 15K008
Basket: 15K0039
Rim Diameter: 1.3 cm
Height: 5.2 cm

119. Miniature Bottle/Ampula.
Probably Abbasid
period.

IAA: 2000-3408
Locus: 17D046;
Basket: 17D0189
Rim Diameter: 1.0 cm
Height: 3.7 cm

Nos.118+120

No. 121

121. Lentoid Pilgrim Flask

IAA: 2000-3634
Locus: 18D070
Basket: 18D0279
Rim Diameter: 1.2 cm
Height: 11.5 cm

LATE ISLAMIC/MEDIEVAL PERIOD

122. Glass Oil Lamp.

IAA: 2000-3693
Locus: 18D070
Basket: 18D0279
Rim Diameter: 6.3 cm
Height: 12.5 cm

No. 122

No. 123

123. Raw Glass for Making Vessels. Late
Islamic/Medieval period. These fragments reveal
the presence of a glass-working atelier in
medieval Banias, where glass vessels and probably other glass objects were made.

IAA: 498059
Locus: 13D010
Basket: 13D0204

THE CATALOG

COINS OF BANIAS

No. 124

124. Coin of King Philip (15/16 C.E.)

Bronze 18mm
Obverse: Head of Tiberius Caesar with countermark
Reverse: Four-columned temple of Augustus at Banias

No. 125

125. Coin of Agrippa II (67–68 C.E.)

Bronze 23mm
Obverse: Head of Nero
Reverse: Inscription in wreath of leaves reading: "Under the Jurisdiction of King Agrippa, Neronias, in the Year 15." Agrippa briefly renamed the city in honor of Nero during the First Jewish Revolt (66–70 C.E.).

No. 126

126. Coin of Agrippa II (78–79 C.E.)

Bronze 21mm
Obverse: Head of Vespasian
Reverse: Tyche (Fortuna), the city's divine patron, stands on a podium, holding a shock of grain in one hand and a horn of plenty in the other. The scene symbolizes great prosperity. The inscription reads: "Year 18 of King Agrippa."

No. 127

127. Coin of Agrippa II (86–87 C.E.)

Bronze 27mm
Obverse: Head of Vespasian
Reverse: Same as 122, but the coin is a larger denomination and the inscription reads: "Year 26 of King Agrippa." The royal palace at Banias was probably under construction at the time these coins were minted.

THE CATALOG

128. Coin of Agrippa II (89–90 C.E.)

Bronze 22mm

Obverse: Head of Domitian

Reverse: Nike, the winged goddess of victory, writes the Roman emperor's name on a shield. The inscription reads: "Year 29 of King Agrippa." The type probably continues to commemorate the Roman victory of the Jews during the First Jewish Revolt (66–70 C.E.).

129. Coin of Marcus Aurelius

Bronze 26mm

Obverse: Head of Marcus Aurelius

Reverse: Zeus stands looking left, with an object, perhaps an altar, at his feet. He holds a wreath or patera (incense shovel) in one hand and a long scepter in the other. Zeus was one of the major deities worshipped in pagan Banias. The coin is dated 172 of the era of Banias, which is the equivalent of 169 C.E. The old mint at Banias seems to have been reopened in that year. The inscription reads: "Caesarea Sebastos, Holy City of Refuge, [situated] before the Panion."

130. Coin of Marcus Aurelius

Bronze 26mm

Obverse: Head of Marcus Aurelius

Reverse: Pan stands with crossed legs, leaning on a tree trunk upon which various objects are hanging. He plays a single-reed flute. This seems to be an actual depiction of the cult statue at the Sanctuary of Pan, which was itself a copy of a work by the classical Greek sculptor Lysippos. The inscription reads: "Caesarea Sebastos, Holy City of Refuge, [situated] before the Panion." It bears the same date as Coin 125 above.

131. Coin of Julia Domna

Bronze 27mm

Obverse: Head of the Empress Julia Domna

Reverse: Tyche (Fortuna), the city's divine patron, stands looking right, holding a ship's prow in one hand and a horn of plenty in the other. She wears a turreted crown (representing the city walls) and a short skirt (called a chilton). This coin probably depicts the actual cult statue in Banias, first set up by Agrippa II. The symbols suggest that the goddess is guarding the city and guiding it to prosperity. The coin is dated 202 of the era of Banias, which is the equivalent of 198/199 C.E. The inscription is the same as Coins 125 and 126 above.

132. Coin of Caracalla (210–211 C.E.)

Bronze 20mm

Obverse: Head of Caracalla

Reverse: The symbols of the city: the syrinx or Pan flute (this one with seven reeds), and a short curved club called a lagobola used by shepherds to kill small animals such as rabbits. The inscription reads: "Caesarea Panias."